50 Steps to Showroom Mastery

A New Way to Sell Cars

Discover How to Supercharge Your Car Sales Career and Become a Showroom Executive

By Gordon Wright, MBA

Dedication

This career guide and sales manual is the detailed guidance I wish I had had when I first got into the car business. It's dedicated to those salespeople who put their customers first and, by doing so, are the true heroes and heroines on the front lines of dealerships across the country. You are the Oxygen of the dealership! Nothing important happens in a dealership until a sale is made. That's why it is so important to learn and implement the best sales practices for the health of your career, the health of the dealership, and the establishment of a base of loyal customers.

If you arrived in your current car sales role by design or by accident, you have probably decided that just "winging it" is not the strategy to guarantee success whether you measure success by large commissions or by an army of loyal fans and advocates. The truth is that you can have both.

In this training manual you will discover and learn the principles and approaches you need to build a new and successful career in the car business. Ten years of working this system in the dealership showroom before, during, and after the global financial crisis (2007-2009) has proved that you can sell more cars and deal with fewer objections if you follow these *50 Steps to Showroom Mastery*. There's a *New Way to Sell Cars*. It's time for you to reach your potential and *Discover How to Supercharge Your Car Sales Career and Become a Showroom Executive*.

How to Use This Guide

Getting Started

Congratulations on stepping up to the challenge of taking control of your career in car sales. Whether you've just started in the business or you have a year or two under your belt and still need to find your rhythm, this book can be the lifeline you need to move quickly to the status of high-level performer.

This "50 Steps" course should be viewed in its 5 components. To get the maximum benefit from this program you should <u>read and start implementing each of the 5 components before moving on to the next</u>. Read, re-read and implement the lessons in Part 1 (the first 10 Steps) and do the same for each 10-Step segment. Spend at least one week on each Part and in 5 weeks, you will have established the momentum to launch your car sales career.

So, let's get started...

Table of Contents   Page

Set Goals

• Working without goals is the best way to guarantee you will struggle to achieve even <u>average</u>

"Begin with the end in mind" ~ Stephen Covey

Goals focus your mind and keep you alert to opportunities. If you keep working from opening to closing without any goals, you will never achieve real success (however you define "success" in your own mind). In sales, results determine your pay and you can decide what your pay will be by setting goals that deliver the results you want. Setting goals (and tracking your progress) allows you to see if something is working or not. Set goals, set a time frame, and track your results. You'll soon realize whether you're growing as a salesperson or not. But you must set goals and they must be specific, measurable, achievable and time-based. Setting goals will provide a clear path to where you want (and need) to be.

Assignment: Get an index card (or use the Notes feature on your smartphone) and write 3 sales goals for this week. Check at the end of each day to see how you are progressing toward the weekly goals, how you made progress, what helped you, what got in the way, and what will you have prepared for tomorrow to keep the momentum going. **Tip**: Make the goals achievable (for you) because you want 3 wins every day (not 3 sales) to keep yourself motivated. Here are three <u>examples</u> (as an illustration) that a car sales professional might use:

1. I will meet with 15 prospects this week (3 per day)

2. I will learn, memorize, and practice one new closing technique (1 per day)

3. I will personally contact 3 people each day (friends, family, past customers, prior unsold prospects) and ask how they are doing, what's new in their lives, and if they know someone currently in the market for a new or used vehicle.

Two

Assume Everyone is Here to Buy

• Pre-qualifying your customers by concluding which ones are not buyers will doom you to sales mediocrity

"Don't build roadblocks out of assumptions" ~ Lorii Myers

If you were in the car business prior to the 2008 financial crisis, you may have experienced a portion of the showroom traffic being "tire kickers" as information was difficult to get unless you visited a dealership. Another portion of the traffic then were "shoppers". Even if you could spot these people (and I believe that's doubtful), the Internet has changed that totally. Almost everyone arriving at a dealership showroom is a buyer and <u>most are looking for someone to take them seriously and "wow" them</u> by making a compelling case to finalize their car-buying project TODAY! If you keep guessing which customers are here to buy and which are not, you're deceiving yourself. The fact is that <u>every customer is here to buy</u>. But the question is, are they here to buy from you? Stop judging every customer and focus and treat every prospect as if they are here to buy a vehicle. Your job is to convince them to buy <u>your</u> product, from <u>your</u> dealership— and from <u>you</u>!

Assignment: Work on changing your mindset and the limiting beliefs that are holding you back from achieving your potential. Visualization can be a powerful way of rewiring your brain. Take time each day to vividly imagine (or remember) an "unlikely" prospect who gradually was moved from "just looking" to being interested to being excited by the possibility of owning the vehicle you are presenting. Maxwell Maltz (in his book Psycho-Cybernetics) revealed that your brain cannot tell the difference between something vividly imaged and something that has actually happened. <u>Start a daily ritual</u> that includes mentally walking through a successful sales process with a casual prospect and re-live the experience of making that sale. First, become a winner in your own mind and it will start to become easier to do in the showroom.

Three

Stay out of The Huddle

. Go to work to work

"Don't get caught up in the unprofessional actions or reactions of others" ~ Angela Scott Moore

In car sales, you are quickly introduced to "the huddle". The huddle is a bunch of salespeople hanging around and doing everything that doesn't involve selling a vehicle. In my first car sales job, I discovered that the top salesperson at the dealership rarely chatted with the other salespeople. He was constantly on the phone talking with past clients or following up with recent visitors. That year, he sold 367 cars (no fleet deals). The crazy thing was, his vehicle presentation skills were average and his product knowledge was not strong. The difference between him and the others who struggled to sell 100 cars in a year was that he came to work to work. The lesson: Stop wasting your time and instead, focus on what you need to do to stay in front of past customers and prospects. Nothing productive ever comes out of the huddle.

Assignment: You don't need to be antisocial but begin excusing yourself from idle "water cooler" sessions and begin planning your day around prospecting for new business, following up with past contacts and customers, and setting up your deliveries to be awesome experiences for your customers. (More tips on these areas later in the course).

Stop Justifying Average Sales

• *Working Hard Enough?* *Doing the Right Work?*

"A fool thinks himself to be wise, but a wise man knows himself to be a fool" ~ William Shakespeare

Selling well is challenging and it takes courage to admit that you are responsible for the results you are achieving (or not achieving). And, it's easy for me to say "Stop making excuses and blaming everything and everyone else for your lack of sales", however, blaming others or your circumstances puts you in a denial mindset that makes the situation completely hopeless. If you are reading this, it's likely that you are justifying average sales by blaming <u>yourself</u>. So the question is, what are you going to do about it? Perhaps you believe or realize that:

- ***You Aren't Working Hard Enough.*** It's an act of courage and bravery to admit this but it's also the first step to remedying this shortcoming. The solution is to commit to doing the <u>things that are known to produce results</u> like arriving at the dealership well before your shift starts, eliminating the weapons of mass distraction that derail your focus, and set personal activity goals each week.

- ***You Aren't Doing the Right Work.*** If you are working hard and not getting the results, you may be doing things that feel like sales work but are simply order taking. Are you working diligently on prospects that arrive at your desk but you avoid the work of prospecting? Are you getting dragged into operational activities that help the dealership and others but do not generate sales for <u>you</u>? It's easy to fill your time doing things that are appreciated by the dealership and your colleagues but keep you from getting closer to your next sale.

Assignment: Identify those activities that cannot be connected to selling and eliminate them or delegate them to someone else. Call a few past customers each day and ask about something related to their family, job, and the vehicle they bought that ties to information that came out of your conversations during the sale. Ask if they have had any <u>conversations</u> recently with friends or colleagues thinking of buying a car. Make it short and friendly. Do it regularly and you will be remembered.

Five

Understand Today's Customers
• *Put Yourself in Your Customers' Shoes*

"It is so much easier to put yourself in your customers' shoes and try to understand how you might help them before they ask for help, than it is to try to mend a broken customer relationship" ~ Mark Cuban

The Internet and smartphones have made consumers better educated today than they were in the past. They have the power to compare prices, to access consumer information and to know their options. The modern consumer wants three things—value for money, service, and custom solutions. Because a car is normally the second biggest purchase the average person makes, they want value to justify their purchase. They want great service - something that is extremely important to today's customers - because they don't have time to sort out every issue or problem that arises. People are more educated and more flexible too. They have many options and can make decisions at many levels, so they want custom solutions.

Assignment: Pretend you are starting the process of buying a car for yourself (and you're not in the business). What steps will you take, where will you search online for information to get a short list of vehicles, and what are you discovering as you put yourself in the customer's shoes? Call or email a few dealerships to inquire about a (competitive) vehicle and see how you are treated. Take what you find as fuel to rethink your approach with prospects and start to orchestrate how you engage with customers to make the car buying process friction-free.

Six

Understand Your Purpose as a Salesperson

• *Focus on Providing a "Dream Come True" Experience*

"Just find your purpose; understand that you have one life to live" ~ Trevor Jackson

To be successful in today's information and option-rich market, you must inspire confidence in the consumer with your <u>enthusiasm for the product</u> and your <u>expert knowledge</u>. This means being positive about what you do every day. You must be able to communicate with customers. This means proper, informed, and persuasive language that will lead customers to a sale. You must have in-depth knowledge about the products that you present as well as those of your competitors. You must also develop the ability to manage

—

buyer tension. This includes being non-confrontational and relating to the customer's needs. When you encounter a customer for the first time in the showroom, the customer's tension relative to you, the sales process, and the chances of being pressured into a buying decision are high. Their tension (and excitement) about the product at that point is low. Your role is to reduce the sales process related tension and increase the product related tension (excitement) so the customer enthusiastically embraces your proposal. We are all different and when it comes to buying cars, so are our customers but they all have these traits in common. Every situation will be different in some respects and there are no quick methods or scripts that work all the time. The key is to use ideas and principles that line up with your approach and belief system and then modify them to your personality.

Assignment: Change or modify your Meet and Greet process to lower tension and get customers comfortable. Move them to your desk to get them talking about their transportation situation. This is the opportunity to get basic information about them put on your worksheet or entered into your CRM. Make sure your desk is inviting. Be a good host: offer refreshments (coffee, tea, water), have a dish of wrapped candies on your desk, have your "brag book" handy, display any of your dealership awards, and have at least one family or friend related picture, You want to demonstrate that this is going to be a very pleasant experience.

Seven

Start Thinking Like a Business Person

• *You're Running a Store Within a Store*

"Sales is really the most noble part of the business because it's the part that brings the solution together with the customer's need" ~ Greg Gianforte

When you're an automotive salesperson, <u>you truly are in business for yourself</u>. You have a storefront (the dealership showroom) and advertising that is bringing customers to the store. The great thing about it is that you don't have to pay for these expenses. Perhaps that's why it is easy for a car salesperson to not take this traffic seriously. Just because you are not paying your own money to acquire the prospects that visit your store doesn't mean you can or should take them for granted. You need to act as though these prospects were generated by your efforts and money and do whatever it takes to move them through the sales process. Treat them like gold. Adjust your mindset and <u>act like you are the owner of the dealership</u>. That mindset means taking pride in the dealership (people and facilities). If you were the owner, you would be quick to show prospects the great team that will be at their service during their ownership, you would be happy to show off your customer lounge, shuttle service, Parts counter, and the shop, as well as introduce them to Service Advisors and the Service Manager.

Assignment. Think and <u>act like you own the dealership</u> by talking to your Service Manager, Parts Manager, and Sales Managers and document some basic statistics about the dealership such as number of technicians, their certifications, size of the Parts Department, the services provided to customers and the equipment and refreshments in the customer lounge to make a visitor's stay enjoyable. Use this information in your Meet & Greet conversation with visitors.

Eight

Understand the "Numbers Game"

• *Many Ways to Impact the Numbers*

"If you do a good job, the numbers say so. You don't have to ask anyone or play politics. You don't have to wait for the reviews" ~ Sandy Koufax

The "old school" sales theory says that the simplest way to increase your income is to increase your numbers. Let's say last month you've seen 50 prospects and sold 10 vehicles. That's a 20% closing ratio. So in order for you to sell 20 vehicles, you would have to see 100 customers. We both know that 50 additional prospects are not going to magically appear in the showroom next month. The smarter way (in the short run) to sell more vehicles is to improve your selling skills. Part of doing that is to start thinking about <u>how to add value for your customers at every step of the sales process</u>. What resources can you create and use to educate your prospect? For example, can you guide your customer through a discussion of whether it makes more sense for them to lease or finance their next vehicle? What are the common problems, questions, and transportation dilemmas you find with the people you meet in the showroom? Start solving people's problems and you will close more sales. So it's not a numbers game. It's a <u>proficiency game</u>.

Assignment: Take 20 minutes to write down all the different types of difficulties, questions, misunderstandings, and outright myths that prospects bring to you during an average month. Start working out answers and solutions (in writing) with information and insights that you can present to customers in these various areas. Even just spending time thinking through <u>how to help customers be better car shoppers and buyers</u> will improve your sales presentations and your sales results.

Track Your Daily Activities

• *Start by Understanding Where You Are Now*

"Even if you're on the right track, you'll get run over if you just sit there" ~ Will Rogers

Sales is, in fact, a numbers game but only to the extent that <u>knowing your current numbers</u> is critical to improving them. For example, have you collected enough data on your own sales results to know your closing ratio on first visit, on be-backs, on phone ups, and on Internet leads? How do you compare to industry averages or your sales team colleagues? Get a week or a month of data at least and see what you are good at. Work on improving the things you are already good at. Once you find a way to track all of your selling activities, you will find your benchmark and be in a position to improve your results because they will tell you where you are doing well and where you need improvement. Keep track of what you do every day so you can understand which areas you need to improve to sell more vehicles.

Assignment: Use a spreadsheet (or your dealership CRM) to track the following and review the totals weekly:

• How many contacts you make each day (walk ups, phone ups, referrals, etc.)

- How many customers gave their information (email, cell number)

- How many presentations you gave

- How many demo drives you went on

- How many sales you closed

- How many vehicles you delivered

Ten

Invest Time in Your Career

. Understand That an Expense Differs from an Investment

"Take time to sharpen the saw" ~ Stephen Covey

Chances are, out of an 8 or 9 hour workday, you only truly work a few hours. Ordering lunch and hanging out in service or the huddle do not count as work. If you put a clock on your daily activities, you might discover that you only really work 3 hours a day in your 8-hour shift. If you were to put the effort into truly working 5 hours a day, you probably would have been able to sell twice the number of vehicles last month. If this sounds crazy, take some time out every day to seriously acquire product knowledge. Read your product manuals with the objective of <u>finding what everyone else has</u>

missed. How would you use your product knowledge to move a customer from one trim level to the next? What does it cost to move from one trim level to the next and do you think the extra features are worth it? Think about what various types of customers would think about the value difference versus the price difference. Critically compare your product to your competitors' and discover where you have the edge. Purchase a course or a book on selling. Whatever it is you're doing at work, just be productive by doing something that will help you sell more vehicles. These first ten steps form a base foundation for what's to come in the rest of the series. Please thoroughly read Steps 1 through 10 of the series and do the assignments to fully understand how to adjust your mindset to become the "showroom executive" of your dealership.

Assignment: Your homework is to take a sheet of paper and draft a weekly schedule for the time you are at the dealership. Carve out time that you reserve for yourself to implement the learning and business development activities we have discussed in Part 1 of this series. Become a product expert and understand your numbers so you can move to improve the aspects of your sales process that are keeping you from achieving the results you need.

Congratulations on completing Part 1 of this career guide. Next up is Part 2 of this five-part guide. In Part 2, you will learn a lot more hands-on techniques that you can start using immediately to improve your sales and income. Time now to pause and review what you have learned so far and make sure you are actually <u>putting these techniques into practice</u>.

Choose the Right Type of Customers
• *Sort and Sift to Identify the Most Productive Customers*

"The wrong person won't be persuaded by anything" ~ Perry Marshall

If you keep working with just walk-in customers, you'll have the toughest time closing a sale. Working with productive customers can literally double, if not triple, your monthly sales and income. When I say productive customers, I don't mean lookers, shoppers and credit criminals. Instead, I mean customers such as repeat customers, referrals, be-backs and phone-ups. These groups of customers have a much higher closing ratio. Depending on which statistics you choose to believe, walk-in prospects can be closed on the same day at 15% to 25% on average on first visit. If you have a customer-centered and consistent follow-up system for the 75% to 85% who did not buy, the broad-based averages say that even though one-third will never come back, about 35% of the remainder will return and <u>about half</u> will buy for a total closing ratio on floor traffic of 30%. The point is you need a lot of fresh floor traffic or tremendous selling skills (or both) to make a living from floor traffic alone particularly in a time when dealership visits are declining with car shoppers doing more of their research online.

Assignment: Use the tracking data you assembled in *Lesson 9* to determine your closing ratio on floor traffic over the past month. Make sure you log everyone you talk to and code them as a Walk-in (Fresh Up), a Be-Back (from an earlier visit), a Phone Lead (who visited as a result of your phone conversation), or a Repeat/Referral customer. Keep track of the sales you close, log each sale under one of these categories, and review your numbers weekly and monthly. If you met with 20 people during the week and sold 5, your overall closing ratio (as a percentage) is 5/20=25%. But, let's say 15 of those 20 visits were Walk-ins and you sold 2 of them, your first time Walk-in closing ratio would be 2/15=13.3%. In this scenario, your other 3 sales came from the 5 other categories, i.e., a ⅗=60% closing ratio. Use your own numbers and prove to yourself what kind of traffic is most productive.

Twelve

Engage and Build Rapport
• *The Pre-Requisite to Asking for the Sale*

"The most effective forms of human intelligence collection are rapport-building and direct questioning" ~ Chelsea Manning

---

Tell me if you've seen this happen in the showroom; a prospect enters and is met by a salesperson that asks, "What prompted your visit today?" and the prospect says, "I am looking at the Nissan Sentra" (substitute your brand). The rookie salesperson (wanting to be helpful) will jump right to their inventory and start presenting the Sentra. Now, if you've been selling cars for even a few weeks, your Sales Manager has probably told you to begin by slowing things down and find common ground with the customer. I do not like the term "slowing things down" but you'll have a much easier time closing the sale later in the process if you engage with the customer in an effort to understand their transportation situation. Your first job is to build a ton of rapport so the customer will trust what you are saying before you move on to presenting the vehicle. Asking questions in a conversational manner and showing genuine interest in the customer's situation is the best way to build rapport.

Assignment: Start making a habit of transitioning your prospects to a conversation about their current transportation early in the Meet & Greet phase. When did they get it? What trips or activities was it used for most often? What did they like about it? What is causing them to consider replacing it? Out of these questions will come some interesting conversations as well as all the information you will need to sell them the right car today!

Easy Ways to Build Rapport
• *Ask Questions to Truly Understand*

"Whether it's at work or with your family. Every minute should be enjoyed and savoured" ~ Earl Nightingale

Everyone is in a rush today and the "old-school" approach of "slowing down the customer" often gets salespeople thinking that engaging in small talk is the way to build rapport. Now, this will work with <u>some</u> clients but not most. So how do you build rapport and keep the process moving at a pace that keeps the customer engaged? The key is to make sure the friendly, rapport-building conversation with the prospect centers around their current vehicle and why it is no longer cutting it for them. You must <u>transition the conversation to their current vehicle</u> no matter how old it is. There are many stories connected to that car that will provide the information and insights you will need to offer a solution to their transportation problem (because that's what you do: <u>help solve customers' transportation problems</u>). Here's what to ask:

- What vehicle are you driving now? Those were great cars. Can I take a quick look at it?

- What has the car been primarily used for?

- What have you liked most about this vehicle?

- How is it not meeting your needs any longer?

- What are you hoping to have in your next vehicle?

Ask a Lot of Questions
. *More Questions Reveal Motivations*

"The art and science of asking questions is the source of all knowledge" ~ Thomas Berger

It's been said that the person who is asking the questions is in charge of the conversation. So if you want to be managing the interaction, be the person asking the questions. If you just stand there only answering all the questions that your customer asks, the customer will soon leave. Why? Because you've provided them with everything they **wanted to know.** <u>But you did not help them discover what they **needed** to know</u>. Asking questions will allow you to discover the customer's needs and **wants**. And, in the end, *what people discover they <u>want</u> is a much more powerful purchase motivator than what they need*. When you ask questions, you open up the possibility of building rapport as clients appreciate your interest in their circumstances and taking them seriously. Your efforts to understand their needs (and wants) will build rapport and trust.

21

Assignment: Besides moving to a new mindset where you ask questions because you are curious about what really brought the customer into your store, make sure you <u>get into the habit of confirming that you truly understand what the customer is saying by repeating back their questions, concerns, and plans.</u> For example, ***"So let me make sure I understand what you are saying, Ms. Customer. Your 1999 Honda Civic has been a great car but it is costing money in repairs lately and, with your two kids in hockey and soccer, you need a newer, more reliable vehicle with enough space to fit all the sports equipment. Is that right?"*** Your customer will interpret this to mean that you really are listening and are making the effort to get her exactly what she wants.

Fifteen

Hot Buttons

• *Revealing Buying Motives*

"Actions are visible, though motives are secret" ~ Samuel Johnson

Hot buttons are basically the customer's buying motives. You must figure out <u>what moves your customer</u>. Listen closely to the customer and look for clues to figure out the customer's buying motives. Normally the important "hot buttons" are two or three of the following issues:

> ***Safety***. Crash test ratings, crash avoidance technologies, safety related design features

Performance. Horsepower & torque, handling dynamics, ride quality, turning circle, towing capacity, and payload

Appearance. Styling & design, the design theme for the brand, relation to concept cars

Comfort/Convenience. Driver ergonomics, thoughtful convenience features, attention to detail

Economy. Gas mileage, overall cost of ownership, Consumer Reports ratings

Durability. Comprehensive and powertrain warranty, retained value, type/quality of materials

The above are the top six buying motives a customer will have when it comes to purchasing a vehicle. Notice the word "price" is not up there. It's because price ranks much lower among hot buttons. Stop trying to sell on price. Figure out what hot buttons move the customer and focus on building value around those issues when presenting the vehicle.

Assignment: Craft your *High Impact Vehicle Presentation* to include these six topics as separate modules. Build and rehearse each presentation module so you can quickly adapt your presentation to focus on those topics and issues that truly matter to the customer. When doing your presentation, just be sure that the key hot button topics are covered in some depth and only touch on (or even eliminate) the topics that are not of concern to the customer.

Sixteen

How Much Product Knowledge Do You Need?

• *More than You Think*

"People who think they know everything are a great annoyance to those of us who do" ~ Isaac Asimov

Set aside some time **every day** to learn product knowledge. Of course, you need to know enough about your product to answer every question and concern the customer might have. However, you must also know what the competitive vehicle has (and does not have) compared to your vehicle. Believe me, most people you meet in the showroom have done enough research to know about the basics of your vehicle and they probably have another brand on their consideration list. Your job is to point out the features your car has that are missing on the competitive vehicle and why that should be important. You need to find a few things about your vehicle that move it to the top of the customer's list. Is it the only car in its segment with _____? If so, that fact needs to be in every presentation with *a story about the importance of that feature*. When you present the vehicle, avoid the temptation to do a "data dump" of everything you know about the car. If it's not relevant, you will just bore the customer. Instead focus on telling them about <u>features that are in alignment with their buying motives</u> (hot buttons).

Assignment. <u>Create a story</u> around each key hot button feature that sets your vehicle apart from the competition. For example, "This is the only compact car on the market with rain-sensing wipers and a customer of mine was telling me recently about how this feature probably saved her life when a transport truck passed her on the highway while hitting a large puddle. Before she could react to the blinding spray, the wipers jumped into action and cleared the windshield immediately!" People remember stories and forget a list of facts. <u>Build your presentation on compelling stories</u> and sell more cars!

Seventeen

F.B.I. Presentations
• *Feature, Benefit, Impact*

"What features your customers ask for is never as interesting as why they want them"
~ Alan Cooper

When you know what the customer needs (and wants), it's time to present the vehicle. But you have to do it in a fashion that builds value in your product. If you build enough value in the product, the price will justify itself. Value building presentations are those that <u>relate the vehicle's characteristics to the issues that the customer has indicated (either directly or indirectly) are most important</u> to him/her. Here's how to structure the components of your presentation:

F- Feature (Name the feature and tell them what it is)

B- Benefit (Explain to them what it does in plain language)

I- Impact (Why they should care and how it affects them)

Remember to concentrate on features that relate to their buying motives (the "hot buttons" you discovered in your initial Meet & Greet and Discovery phase). Whether the features you identify are unique to your brand or not is less important than the story you tell around each one that helps the customer imagine how each feature is going to be important in their life with this vehicle. For example, an SUV with a hands-free automatic tailgate (***Feature***) means that when you arrive at the vehicle with arms full of groceries, you can access the storage area with ease (***Benefit***). This eliminates one of life's frustrations and we could all do with a little less stress in our lives (***Impact***). This would be one of your Comfort/Convenience hot buttons.

Assignment. Go through the features of your top selling vehicle and write down the important features using the Hot Buttons categories covered in Step 15. Record the Feature, Benefit, and Impact for each hot button topic. Remember that most examples can be used on multiple vehicles or trim levels. The Safety features available on one model in your lineup will be the same as for other models so (unless a feature is unique to a particular vehicle) you can use the same "FBI" story across the product line.

Eighteen

Going on Demonstration Drives

. Who Drives First?

"Cars are the sculptures of our everyday lives"
~ Chris Bangle

Always remember that your objective is to <u>do everything possible to sell a car today</u> to the prospect in front of you. Everyone should get the ***V.I.P. Presentation***. Avoid the temptation to "phone it in". There are those salespeople who hand the customer the keys and say, "See you back in 15 minutes." But, that's not you! **You must go on the demo drive**. Common sense tells you that <u>the vehicle won't sell itself.</u> All this time, you presented the vehicle by telling them everything they needed to know about it. Now it's time for them to <u>experience it themselves</u> and confirm what you have been telling them. Have pre-planned routes so you know where you are going. Have a few different routes if possible. Plan for:

- Straight roads - demo acceleration & braking

- Stop and go traffic - demo visibility, blind spots, safety systems

- Roads with lots of bends and turns - demo handling & cornering

- Freeways - demo passing, automatic cruise control, ride quality

Don't just go around the block and come back in 5 minutes. Take as long as it takes to sell the vehicle. **A quick tip:** On the way back from the demo drive, be quiet. Don't say anything unless asked and let the customer build <u>mental ownership</u> of the vehicle.

Nineteen

Presenting in the Middle of the Demo Drive

• *Test Drive Pattern Interrupt*

"Salesmanship is limitless. Our very living is selling. We are all salespeople" ~ James C. Penney

Some sales trainers suggest it might be better for you to present the vehicle in the middle of the demo drive. I believe that (having selected a vehicle you believe will be the perfect fit for the customer) you should provide enough of a presentation at the dealership (either in the showroom or at the vehicle before you head out on the test drive) to prepare the customer for what they will be experiencing, as well as highlighting some of the main reasons why this vehicle should be at the top of their consideration list. Whether all or some of the presentation is done halfway through the demo drive is less important than how this approach can add some **dramatic emphasis** to your pitch.

Assuming weather conditions are accommodating, pull over in an empty parking lot and do your presentation at about the halfway point. (This is also the appropriate time to switch drivers if you have two family members who will be driving the new car). The advantage you have at this point is that your customers are getting used to the vehicle and are probably more relaxed than they were back at the dealership. You may find them more receptive to your proposal. This way, when you present the vehicle, there are fewer distractions. You also will not be competing with other salespeople trying to present the same vehicle in the showroom.

Twenty

Who Drives First?
• *Reducing Test Drive Anxiety*

"Selling is something we do for our clients - not to our clients" ~ Zig Ziglar

Most sales trainers teach this and I have found it usually works better if the <u>salesperson drives first</u> on the demonstration drive. The customer is not familiar with the vehicle, so you should drive for the first few minutes. You can then pull over at a safe pre-determined spot and switch drivers (which might also be the perfect time to do a presentation). Some customers are not comfortable with taking a demo drive. But if you want to sell the car to them, they must drive it. And you driving first is the perfect way to set this up. Also, if you demonstrate the vehicle's quick acceleration in the first couple of minutes, the customer will feel less reluctant to put the vehicle through its paces when it's their turn to drive. After all, building excitement about the vehicle and its capabilities is what you want. Just remember that for some customers (not looking for a sports car experience), too much excitement may not help you close the deal.

Tip: Every person with a valid driver's license in the car should drive. This way, you keep everyone involved and at the same time, build more mental ownership.

Some of the ideas we listed above are pretty basic, so consider this a refresher course. If you don't have the basics down, you will never profit from moving on to the more advanced techniques found in the last three sections of this course.

The key to a successful automotive sales career isn't always knowing everything. As a matter of fact, you could know every single trick in the book and still not sell a single car. It is the **DOING** that turns you into a showroom superstar in this business.

In Part 3 of this guide (Chapters 21 to 30), you will learn a lot more hands-on techniques that you can start using immediately to improve your sales and income. In the meantime, you need to keep on reviewing and putting into practice the information you have learned to this point.

The Service Walk

• *Setting the Post-Sale Image*

"If you lack the courage to start, you have already finished" ~ Joe Girard

A service walk is a great idea to build value in your dealership but most salespeople do the service walk only at the time of delivery. It's a good thing if you do the service walk at delivery, but why not do it as part of your regular sales process? I always found it was easiest and most effective to include the service walk as part of the vehicle presentation. When you present the vehicle, go right in and show the customer the whole facility and introduce them to your service advisors and managers. The other most natural time is upon returning from a demo drive. The service walk should include the customer lounge and the helpful services available (free Wi-Fi, free refreshments, children's play area, re-charging station, etc.). Don't forget the Parts Department (better to call it the Accessories Store). Be proud of the place you work at and don't give up another chance to brag about (and build value in) your dealership.

Assignment. Meet with your Service Manager to assemble some basic facts about your service operation. For example, how many licensed technicians, how many apprentices, number of service bays, special equipment and technologies, and regular programs for customers (such as free car wash with each service visit) are questions you should be able to answer even though the customer has not specifically asked. Prepare a 60 second profile that includes some "wow" facts that you can use to dazzle customers, for example, "**We have 5 Master Technicians on our team who have over 10 years experience servicing our brand of vehicle**". Your short but impactful service walk presentation must leave your prospective customer feeling that this is a dealership I can trust to provide an outstanding post-purchase experience.

Show Some Hospitality
• *Treating a Client Like a Guest*

"Hospitality: making your guests feel like they're at home, even if you wish they were" ~ Justine Vogt

Hospitality is part of building a great first impression. If you think about your prospect customer as your Guest, you will be looking for ways to show hospitality. If you're passing by a vending machine at your dealership, stop and buy your customers a beverage. Or if they have kids, purchase them a snack. If you're on a demo drive and you're passing by a coffee shop, stop and take out a few bucks and buy your customers something. Don't be cheap.

Demo drives are the best chance to stop for food and build more rapport with your customers. Consider these as small investments in the relationship. I guarantee the few bucks you spend will only increase your chance of closing the sale and earning a commission.

Assignment. To the extent that your dealership policies permit, make your desk a hospitable place. Have quick access to bottled water that you can offer. I also made sure I always had a dish of wrapped hard candies on my desk (regular and sugar-free, of course). A small sweet makes it easier to close the sale if your prospect skipped lunch and needs a boost to complete the deal.

Twenty-three

"Park in the Sold Section" Close
• *Here's a Better Trial Close to Wrap Up the Demo Drive*

"Opportunities don't happen. You create them" ~ Chriss Grosser

There is a moment when you return from the test drive that is particularly critical to moving the process forward toward a positive outcome. Some "old school" sales types will suggest you use the "Park in the Sold Section" Close at this point. (This is where you ask the prospect to park the car in the Sold Section and then try to deal with the objections that are raised). I disagree with this approach (although, it will work sometimes) in favour of something more forthright and more likely to determine where you stand before moving to presenting numbers. There is no point in presenting financial offers unless the prospect is relatively enthusiastic about the vehicle being considered. Here's how you can get an honest assessment from your prospect and what to do with it:

- When you return and the vehicle has stopped, ask your customer, "So, Ms. Customer, let me ask you.... On a scale of 1 to 10, "10" meaning it's the perfect vehicle for you and you should own it today, or "1", meaning it's a piece of junk and should be headed for the scrap yard.... How would YOU rate the car as the right one for you?"

- If you get a response of 8 or better, it means they want the vehicle and you should say, *"Wow. That's a great score. What would make it a 10?"*

- If you get a 7 or less, something major is wrong and you must say *"That certainly won't work. What would make the vehicle a 10?"*

I have used this close hundreds of times and customers <u>always</u> give me a number. And you have some information about what is needed to get the number to 10 that you can use in designing an offer. If the answer is 9 or 10, the car is effectively <u>sold</u> and 8 probably means some accessory or package needs to be added. Let the customer tell you exactly what would make it perfect and close on that. Now <u>you have a commitment</u> (and you haven't even started talking about the numbers). Master this simple close and watch your sales and income grow.

Twenty-four

Involving Your Prospects in the Trade-in Evaluation

. *Buy Their Car to Sell Yours*

"Stop selling, start helping" ~ Zig Ziglar

I have always found that getting the customer involved in a discussion of their trade-in vehicle **early in the process** is the best way to establish rapport, trust, and a belief by the customer that you have their interest in mind. Talking about the vehicle being replaced also provides you with lots of information that will be needed in selecting a replacement vehicle. You will be filling out an appraisal sheet to give to your manager, so make sure you have a clipboard handy to do the appraisal <u>at the vehicle</u> <u>with your customer</u> and have your customer assist you as follows:

1. Have them remove their old car keys from their house keys

2. Ask them to read you the mileage from their old car

3. Ask them to read you the VIN number of the vehicle

Get the customer involved as well by asking questions, e.g., ***"Has the vehicle been involved in any collisions? Any rust proofing done on the vehicle? Are you the original owner? Any money still owing on the vehicle?"*** Make them feel as if they are <u>selling</u> their vehicle today (which means they will be buying yours as well). All of these little tips will set a smooth foundation for a great close.

By the way, there are a number of **smartphone apps** that help this process go quicker and smoother by scanning the V.I.N. and taking photos of the vehicle (particularly damaged areas). Use whatever technology your dealership has approved but remember the underlying principle: the trade-in appraisal is the opportunity to manage the sales process more effectively and build a real connection with your prospect early in the process.

How NOT to De-Value the Customer's Trade-in

• *It Costs Nothing to Show a Little Respect*

"Make improvements, not excuses. Seek respect, not attention" ~ Roy T. Bennett

The conventional "old school" wisdom in the car business is to subtly de-value the customer's trade-in because most people over-value their trade-in vehicle. It is certainly important to provide your prospect with a <u>reality check</u>, however, starting from a "de-value" mindset often gets you off on the wrong foot.

Give your prospect something for their vehicle (that doesn't cost you anything). By that I mean, say something like, "***It looks like this minivan holds a lot of memories about times the family spent together. Is that right?***" You see, that didn't cost you anything but it did communicate that <u>you value what their trade-in means to them</u>. It will also spark a conversation about their transportation history and needs.

It still makes sense to touch any dents, scratches, and blemishes without commenting. This is called the **silent walk around** and it always results in your customer giving you an explanation for everything wrong with the vehicle which tells you that the customer is realizing that they won't be selling their trade-in at the top end of the range they had in mind. Your kind and respectful attitude will get you much farther than an approach that could be interpreted as arrogant and demeaning.

Twenty-six

Planting Seeds for Your Finance Manager
• *Letting the Customer Take Ownership*

"Life is like a garden, you reap what you sow" ~ Paulo Coelho

Planting little seeds in your customers' minds will increase your backend income and make your Finance Manager happy. If you listen for clues during Discovery, you can find opportunities to drop seeds for a later F&I setup. Don't spend too much time on this matter; rather breeze through it during your presentation just to see if the customer shows interest.

Examples:

- If they have a trade, when you are doing a silent walk around, ask if they had an extended warranty on their trade or had any rust proofing done.

- If they tell you their vehicle was just stolen, tell them about the security system you offer that could have prevented   it.

Every time you get an opportunity to drop a seed, don't miss out. <u>But then, just move on</u>. You don't want to get into a discussion and you don't want to find yourself "selling" these F&I products and services. Remember, **your number one priority is to sell the car**. Focus on selling, but if you find an opportunity to plant a seed, just get it done and quickly move on.

Twenty-seven

Don't <u>**Ever**</u> Leave Your Customer
• *Distractions Can Kill the Sale*

"Engaging people is about meeting their needs — not yours" ~ Tony Robbins

The one point I always dreaded in the sales process was the short period of time I needed to leave my customers to get numbers from the Desking Manager. I knew that every minute my customer was alone was a minute that they could start to have second thoughts. And since smartphones have arrived, it is the opportunity to check competition and even talk to a salesperson at another store. To offset this problem, I hope you are at least offering them coffee or something cold to drink. Offering something to drink will ease their tension a bit.

If your managers are working on numbers for you, <u>come back to the customer and chat and build more rapport with them</u>. Whenever you are not with your customer, make sure they have something to read that builds value in you as a friend in the car business. Having a "brag book" that your customer can flip through is a great way to accomplish this.

The "Brag Book"
• *Your Marketing Vehicle*

"Too many people overvalue what they are not and undervalue what they are" ~ Malcolm Forbes

The idea of creating a "brag book" is not new or unique but so few salespeople invest the time to do it that <u>you will stand out by completing this basic task</u>. Get yourself a 3-ring binder with sheet protectors and place all of your happy customer letters, survey comments, and photos in it. Include all your contact information including social media locations and invite customers to follow you on Facebook, Instagram, Twitter, LinkedIn, etc.

We talked about creating value in yourself, your product and your dealership. Now use your brag book to prove it to them. It doesn't matter what you call your book. <u>Just make sure you create one</u>! Include a brief profile about yourself such as how you got into the car business, what you enjoy most about the business, and your philosophy about how you treat and work with customers. When you are waiting for figures from your manager and you really need to leave your desk, just hand them your book and say, *"**Ms. Customer, I'll be right back. Oh, and by the way, you might want to take a look at this. Plus there is a great article on page 3 about the vehicle you're getting**."*

Great Tip: Try this, it worked great for me. Create a headline with your picture on the cover of the binder with the following title in bold type: **Please DO NOT Buy a Car from Your Name Until You Read This First**! If this is sitting on your desk, people are compelled to open it. When they read and see all the wonderful comments about your work, they will get the joke and appreciate your sense of humour as well as understand why they should be buying their next car from you!

Twenty-nine

Getting Customer Testimonials
• *Social Proof is a Powerful Influencer*

"Nothing ruins your day more than getting a bad review" ~ Taylor Swift

First, do not ask for a testimonial, ask for **feedback**. When you ask for feedback, you can structure the response and make it easier for your customer. Start by asking, *"**Could I get some feedback on your experience here at Tip Top Motors?**"* I always found it was effective to use a short survey to prompt answers that provide credible and persuasive recommendations:

- What problems were you looking to solve when you bought your Nissan Rogue (substitute your make and model)?

- What was it that ultimately made you choose to buy at Tip Top Motors?

- What did you appreciate most about the way your purchase project was handled?

- Would you recommend our dealership and my services to friends and family?

- Any other comments or specific feedback?

The easiest way to get happy customer recommendations is at the time of delivery. Set up these questions on dealership letterhead with lines following each question so customers can hand write their responses.

I always provided an envelope addressed to our General Manager so customers felt that their comments were going directly to the boss (and they did). Make sure to ask permission to use any of their comments in dealership marketing materials and quote directly from the comments received (including spelling and grammar mistakes if any). Also, put these comments in your "brag book".

Thirty

Adding Value to Your Brag Book
• *Self Promotion is Your Duty*

"Many of us have this mind-set which considers self-promotion a taboo" ~ Abhishek Ratna

If you're using a brag book as recommended in Section 26, that's great! If you're not using one, then you need to start right away. Photos are extremely popular with people. And, that's one of the best ways to add more value to your brag book. Buy yourself a digital camera or simply use your smartphone and make it a habit on every delivery to get pictures of your customer standing next to their new vehicle. Include these pictures with your happy customer feedback survey in your book. It's this type of creativity that separates the above average salesperson from the average. But don't stop there.

- Set up an ***Instagram*** account and post your delivery photos.

- If you have a Gmail account, it's easy to set up a YouTube Channel and post short videos of your customers taking delivery and commenting on their car buying experience with you.

Get creative in your selling career and watch yourself turn into a superstar. You really need to start implementing some of these techniques immediately. If they are applied properly, you'll see immediate results.

Great progress! If you have been studying and implementing the lessons in this guide so far, you're over halfway to Showroom Mastery! You'll soon move on to Part 4 of this series. In that portion of the guide, we will reveal how to create a dream-come-true delivery experience for your customer that will set the stage for a lifelong relationship including enough referrals and repeat business to fill your sales pipeline. In the meantime, keep on reviewing and implementing Parts 1, 2 and 3 of this series.

Thirty-one

Prepare for Delivering the Vehicle
. *Setting the Stage for the Big Day*

"Savvy dealerships have discovered that delivering good customer service has a direct impact on their bottom line" ~ Ned Smith

The delivery is actually the very <u>first step to your next sale</u> so make a lasting positive impression on your customers by being prepared. Make sure the paperwork and the vehicle are ready an hour before delivery. Physically check over the entire vehicle to make sure everything is the way it should be (especially while the service department is still open if that is possible).

Everything that was promised in the way of accessories must be installed. Don't wait for the last minute to get things done, or even worse, while the customer is waiting to pick up their vehicle. Consider that your customer, ever since they committed to buying the vehicle, has been eagerly anticipating this day. Any delays or hiccups during the delivery will diminish the thrill of the moment. Even experienced car buyers get a kick out of picking up a new vehicle, so <u>do whatever it takes</u> to make sure the delivery goes off without a hitch.

Detailing & Filling the Tank
• *Sweating the Details*

"If you don't understand the details of your business, you are going to fail" ~ Jeff Bezos

Make sure the vehicle is super clean, detailed and parked in a delivery zone where you have room to walk around the vehicle with the customer. Remember how important first impressions are? So make sure that the vehicle is spotless even if it's a used car or even if you have to pay for the wash personally. Get a supply of micro-fiber cloths and spray polish to do last minute touch ups that the detailer may have missed. Also, it is very important to <u>make sure the gas tank is full.</u> Dealership policies vary, so if the policy is not to have full tanks, take it to the gas station anyway and fill it up. Let your customer know that you filled the tank up for them (whether you filled it or your dealership filled it). Your goal is to dazzle your customer with a vehicle that is spotless, inside and out, and ready to roll.

Thirty-three

Leave a "Goody Bag" in the Car
. It's the Thought That Counts

"A little thought and a little kindness are often worth more than a great deal of money"
~ John Ruskin

Leave a packet for your customer. Use a small size resealable baggie and fill it up with a few things that might be handy to them, such as a small packet of tissues, your business cards, an air freshener, note pad & pencil, and one dollar's worth of change (quarter, dime, nickel)—your customers will love you for getting creative and being considerate. Tesla gives everyone an umbrella, t-shirt, keychain, etc. Be creative and helpful so you will be memorable.

Thirty-four

Introduce Your Customer to the Service Manager
• *The Role of the "Warranty Department"*

"Your main dealer may be just as competitive as the small local garage" ~ Miles Brignall

It's important for your customer to connect with a name and a face in the Service Department because <u>any vehicle-related problem</u> that they might have after they drive off will be an issue <u>best handled by the Service Department</u>.

All new cars (and most used cars) you sell will come with a factory or dealership warranty of some sort. <u>You want any product complaints handled by the people at your dealership who are trained to solve them</u>. If your customers are familiar with the people in your Service Department, they will not bother you with service issues. Let the service department do its job.

I used to <u>introduce the Service Department as the "Warranty Department"</u> to emphasize the role of this department in keeping the customer's vehicle compliant with the factory warranty and taking care of any adjustments that might become necessary under the warranty. This would also imply that the Service Department personnel would <u>act as the</u>

49

customer's advocate in any dealings with the manufacturer about whether a particular repair was covered by the factory warranty.

Asking For & Getting Referrals
. *Become a Hero, Be a Connector*

"Big changes follow from small events" ~ Malcolm Gladwell

A few rules about asking for referrals that you must keep foremost in your mind:

1. People give referrals because it makes them feel good, not as a favour to you.

2. Monetary rewards for personal referrals are usually ineffective (and can be counter-productive).

3. You must be referable to ask for and get referrals.

A lot of car salespeople hesitate to ask for referrals because they feel awkward about asking their customer for a <u>favour</u>. If this is how you feel, it's time to change your mindset. <u>Think about this:</u> if you receive great service and/or a great purchase experience, you___

50

want to share it with friends, family and colleagues. You hope your friend will appreciate your recommendation and find it helpful. You feel good and become a "hero" to your friend when your recommendation results in a positive benefit.

Your customers are motivated in the same way. That's why referral fees have limited impact on your customers' willingness to recommend you. You must build a strong rapport with your customer and then you can ask for a referral. Always ask permission when asking for a referral. (See #29 for additional techniques).

Recommended. A specific wordtrack that you can use at delivery is: "***Ms. Customer, I hope you felt that your buying experience here was positive and that you will not hesitate to recommend my services to friends, family, and colleagues. I will continue to stay in touch with you and I would ask that whenever you are having a conversation where the topic of updating or replacing a vehicle is raised, that you will remember me and introduce me into the conversation***". You then must commit to keeping in touch with your customer so you truly are top-of-mind when someone in their circle is in the market for new transportation.

Thirty-six

Life Long Follow-Ups

. Establishing a Relationship

"The quality of your life is determined by the quality of your relationships" ~ Harvey Mackay

If you have only been in the business a short time, resolve to make continuous follow-up a routine part of how you operate. It will be the difference between an ELF career (easy, lucrative, and fun) and a HALF career (hard, annoying, lame, and frustrating). One of the big differences is Follow-Up (keeping in touch) with your customers for life (i.e., until they die). So, when do you stop following up?

- **When they die.**

- **When they move and you can't get in touch with them.**

- **When their phone and address have changed and there is no way of contacting them.**

- **When they tell you never to call again.**

It's a failed strategy and a waste of time to wait for customers to walk through the door. Instead, follow up and bring people in to see you. Here's how to do it for Sold Customers and Unsold Customers:

Follow-up examples for ***Sold Customers at Delivery***:

- "We are doing a survey here at Tip Top Motors. Can I ask you a couple of questions?"

- "I am updating my records, do you mind if I ask you a couple of questions?"

- "Oh, I almost forgot, can I ask you a couple of questions?"

Once you have permission, use questions such as these:

- "How many vehicles are in your household?"

- "How many of you drive?"

- "Who do you think is next in line for a new or used vehicle?"

- "Is that going to be pretty soon or sometime in the future?" (Either/or question.)

If they are uncertain, just ask, **"If you had to guess?"** This works well for getting an answer out.

Follow-up examples for ***Unsold Customers before they leave***:

- "Before you go, can I ask a couple of quick questions?"

- "Do you think you will be making a decision in a week, a month or more like a year?" (Either/or question.)

Point out that it's tough to buy a vehicle these days. They will probably have many questions and when they get a little closer, you can send them some information on your products, if that's all right. (Make sure you have a valid email address, as an absolute minimum, before your prospect leaves and add them to your email follow up list).

Thirty-seven

Basic **SOLD** Customer Follow-Up Time Line
. *Step-by-Step Process*

"Follow up and follow through until the task is completed, the prize won" ~ Brian Tracy

If your <u>consistently</u> do half of the following activities with everyone you meet at the dealership, you will be ahead of most other salespeople in your industry. If you follow all these suggestions, you will be a **rock star performer**, guaranteed!

• **Text customers within a few hours after delivery.**

• **Send customers a thank you <u>card</u> the same day.**

• **Call customers within 48 hours to see if they have any questions and discover the reaction of friends and family to the new vehicle.**

• **Seven days or a week later, make a second phone call to ask if they have been using the electronics on the vehicle and do they have any questions. (J.D. Power says that 40% of your customers would like a short refresher session on some aspects of the vehicle's electronic technologies).**

• **In 30 days or a month later, make a third phone call. Remind your customer to keep your name top-of-mind and to <u>introduce you into the conversation</u> when the topic of acquiring a new vehicle is part of discussions with friends and colleagues.**

• **Put your customer on your monthly email newsletter list and make sure all past customers get your regular email. (Use an email program such as MailChimp or ConstantContact to add some style and professionalism to your regular communications).**

Among the topics to cover in these follow-up emails and phone calls will be reminders to <u>complete the manufacturer's survey</u> (new car clients), invitations to any upcoming Service Department orientation activities, requests for referral contacts, and offers to do something for them such as add them to your LinkedIn network, or promote their business to your other clients. **Always focus on adding value to any follow-up contact**.

Thirty-eight

Basic <u>**UNSOLD**</u> Customer Follow-Up Time Line

. *Step-by-Step Way to Get Them Back*

"You just can't beat the person who never gives up" ~ Babe Ruth

If your <u>consistently</u> do half of the following activities with everyone you meet at the dealership, you will be ahead of most other salespeople in your industry. If you follow all these suggestions

• Text them within a few hours.

• Email them within 12 hours with a <u>Thanks for Your Visit</u> message.

• Send a Thank You <u>card</u> the same day. You will truly stand out from the crowd.

• Call them every couple days for two weeks (but do not leave messages). Their call display will let them know that you called. If you have important new information that they should be considering, send it in an email.

• Put them on your regular email list. That is, the mailing that goes out every month to update them on new promotions now being run by the dealership or the manufacturer.

• Call them every 60 days just to <u>see how their car-shopping project is going so far</u> and what vehicles are still on their consideration list.

Always focus on **adding value** to any follow-up contact. You don't want to be a pest. You want to be seen as <u>a helpful car shopping resource</u>. Send car review articles, safety ratings, and car buying tips as well as explanations or manufacturer videos about the cool electronics on the vehicle they are considering.

If you're even a little bit creative, use an email service such as **ConstantContact** or **MailChimp** to create professional newsletter-style emails. They have lots of easy to use templates so you can send something appealing that gets through spam filters. You'll also be able to track who has opened your emails and clicked on your links.

Thirty-Nine

Using the Telephone

• *Your Highest Closing Ratio Activity*

"Cold" Calling Might be Dead, But Not Smart Calling" ~ Art Sobczak

I hope you've been trying to change your mix of customer groups. If you don't already know, walk-in customers have the lowest closing ratio. You have a much better shot at closing repeats, referrals and be-backs than any "fresh ups". This alone is a strong reason to focus your follow-up activities on these groups. However, one group that also has a **high closing ratio** is phone-ups. So you now have another target group but <u>you need to learn to get on the phone</u>. Remember that, with most people now owning smartphones and with most dealer websites featuring ***Click-to-Call*** capability, people shopping for a car are now likely to just click that button and ask their questions. So, if you're not racing to the phone for a phone-up, you're throwing money down the drain. Learning to use the phone properly is an investment in your earning power as a sales professional. The difference between making a lot of money in the car business and making none is <u>one appointment per day</u>! Some of the skills you will need to do that are covered next.

Getting a Name & Number from a Phone Up
• *Managing the Conversation*

"High expectations are the key to everything"
~ Sam Walton

Recent research suggests that Phone leads are closer to making a decision than Internet leads, and you should expect to convert 20% to 25% of phone leads into an in-store visit if you follow the process outlined here. **Your sole purpose in handling a phone-up is to set an appointment**. It is not to simply answer the customer's questions over the phone. Here is a basic outline for setting an appointment from a phone call and, at the same time, getting a name and number out of a phone-up for later follow-up.

<u>Greet</u>:

• Greet the customer by giving your name and then by asking, "***How may I assist you today***?"

• Answer any questions the customer asks and keep answering questions.

• <u>Do not answer any questions the customer does not ask</u>! (As soon as you start answering questions that were not asked, you are perceived as "selling").

Close:

• After the customer finishes asking questions, pause and ask **"Tell me, would you like to drive it?"**

• **"Well is 5 pm tomorrow OK or would later be better?"**

Confirm:

• **"Good, I'll see you at the showroom on Thursday at 7:00 pm. By the way, if you're running late, will you call me?"**

• **"And, of course, if something should change here, I 'll return the courtesy; your cell number is?"**

> • **"Again, my name is _____ _____, and you are?"**

If you stick to your old habits, you'll have pretty much what you have now. Try these new techniques and I guarantee a positive change in your percentages. And if the techniques taught here are performed properly, you will be on your way to showroom mastery.

I trust you have now started to develop some new and productive habits that are showing results. Now, before you move on to the 5th part of this series of 50 Steps, pause and take a few days to consider what you have been able to implement so far and how the changes in your routine have started to produce more confidence, more engagement with clients and improved results.

In the upcoming final section of the series, we will talk about building a lifetime career in car sales that will be more lucrative than you thought possible. In the meantime, keep reviewing and implementing everything you have learned in this course so far and tell us about the results at www.ShowroomSalesSkills.com.

Forty-one

Building Your Own Sales Career

. *To build a sales career, build relationships*

"If you are not taking care of your customer, your competitor will" ~ Bob Hooey

The way to build your own sales career is to **build a pipeline full of potential customers** so you never have to wait for a walk-in customer to arrive at the door. If you properly prospect, use the telephone, internet, email marketing and constantly set appointments with your customers, you'll always stay busy and won't have any time to take care of walk-in traffic. **Marketing yourself is your ticket to filling that pipeline**. With the exponential power of digital communications, you can now make ten times the connections that were possible a decade ago when one-to-one communication repeated many times was the only way to generate the numbers needed to fill that pipeline. In this last part of the course, we will review how to insure this continuous funnel of prospects. Just like a healthy business will be generating sales and income streams from several sources, you will be successful by tapping into multiple sources for potential customers. Here are a few outside-the-box approaches that can generate sales streams to your car sales business:

Local businesses. Especially if your dealership sells trucks or commercial vehicles, make sure you are visiting local businesses such as landscapers, delivery businesses like restaurants, and real estate agents who lease vehicles for their sales teams or other business purposes. Make yourself known to local businesses and their employees by visiting with coffee and donuts on a regular basis and invite them to join your V.I.P. club.

Networking. Start with your own network of friends and family and start building relationships with a diverse collection of people in your town or city by joining civic and community groups as well as your local Board of Trade.

Advertise Online. The Internet makes it possible for car sales professionals to get in front of local potential customers at a low cost. Using Facebook and Google AdWords you can target potential customers. Look for a Google-certified professional to handle this targeted digital advertising method and get your phone ringing.

Forty-two

Early-Bird Prospecting

. Pick Up New Customers While the Sales Team is Sleeping

"People will do business with those they know, like, and trust" ~ Bob Burg

Service customers can be a good source of prospects. If you have a service department, you should go in early, right around when it opens. Take some coffee and donuts and give them out in the waiting lounge. Build rapport with the customers and offer a no-obligation presentation of a newly launched model in the showroom or a presentation on a new technology now available on the current model year vehicles. It's great practice and will quickly get you known among dealership customers as the vehicle and tech expert. Ask for referrals every chance you get. Hand out your business card. Your service customers are already doing business with your dealership, so they are an extremely good source of prospects. Turn them into fans and the business will start turning up before you know it.

Forty-three

Prospecting in Your Service Department
. *Pick the Low Hanging Fruit First*

"Proper prospecting prevents poverty" ~ Jeffrey Gitomer

An easy way to build your daily appointments is to use your Service Department. Go into Service and walk up to a Service Advisor. Ask the Service Advisor to hand you at least 3 completed R.O's (Repair Orders) every day. All you have to do is call those 3 customers and ask them how their service experience was with your dealership. Build a ton of rapport with them, set appointments and ask for referrals (use the referral script in #35). Be sure to ask management before you start this, however, because most dealerships require their Service Advisors to do this kind of follow-up anyway, so you would be doing your Service Advisor teammate a big favour. You would be doing the dealership a favour as well.

This technique is one of the simplest ways to build your customer base and have people constantly coming to you to purchase a vehicle. While you are engaged in these conversations with people who are already customers, you will strike up some friendships, learn about some immediate and longer term selling opportunities, and become known to the dealership's customers.

Forty-four

Prospecting by Mail
• *Combining Digital and Analog*

"Listening is the new prospecting" ~ John Jantsch

Despite this digital age, you simply must also prospect by mail. Regular snail mail is so rarely used lately that you will automatically stand out as unique. You become memorable. It is much easier for prospects to remember you if they see your name in writing in a touch-and-feel format. <u>When you combine snail mail, email, text, and phone calls in a way that insures your customers and prospects hear from you at least every 60 days or less, you will soon develop a following that is like owning a gold mine</u>. Here are a few ideas for your direct mail campaign:

- Send birthday cards
- Send holiday cards
- Send cooking recipes
- Send service tips
- Send car wash and detailing tips
- Send Service Department coupons
- Send your personal newsletter. This is the best type of mail to send. Use an email service such as **MailChimp** or **ConstantContact** to create information pieces (such

as the above list) that customers and prospects will find interesting and helpful.

The possibilities are truly endless. It all boils down to your level of creativity. It is not so much what you send; the idea is you must send something so that <u>they will remember you</u>.

Forty-five

Orphan Customers
• *Be Kind to the Homeless*

"Orphan owners from your dealership are a great source of no-cost leads for any car sales professional" ~ Robert Wiesman

If your dealership is well established, then chances are, your dealership has "orphan owners." An "orphan owner" is <u>a customer whose salesperson no longer works at the dealership</u>. These people are a good source of referrals and prospects. All you have to do is call them and inform them that the salesperson who helped them last time with their vehicle purchase is no longer with your dealership and you have been asked to **be their sales contact at the store**. If they have any further questions about their vehicle or another purchase, they now have a new friend in the car business. Also have them write down your name and number and follow up with them by mail and by phone. Follow up by mail every 45 days. Follow up by phone every 60 days. There is a pretty good chance that this level of attention is more than what they got from their original salesperson.

Seal the connection by sending a card and email letting them know that you will continue to be in touch from time to time with information that they should find helpful in making the most of their car ownership experience.

Forty-six

Using the Online Phone Book

• *Target Neighbours of Sold Customers*

"A lumpy envelope is always intriguing" ~ Dee Black

Here is a great little strategy that can be very effective called "411 Marketing". Get a list of recent dealership customers (or your own sold customers) and look up their addresses online. In the US, use www.phonebooks.com and in Canada, use www.Canada411.ca. Use your local postal codes or zip codes to search for **addresses that are right around your customers' homes**. Write a very personalized, compelling letter (or postcard) and mail it to them. Make the message extremely personalized (hand-written works best), and tell the prospect in the letter/card that you heard that they were in the market for a new or used vehicle. (Mention that one of your recent customers is a neighbour).

Just introduce yourself and let them know that they have a friend in the car business. If your letter is well written and very personalized, the results can be terrific. Send out 3 of these letters every day. This should get your phone ringing with new prospects.

Note: Please check your local post office to comply with mail-out laws before you try this. To send out pre-printed (less personalized) over-sized postcards in the US, use **Every Door Direct Mail** (<u>EDDM</u>) to target specific zip codes and income/age demographics within each zone. In Canada, use **Canada Post's** <u>SmartMail</u> marketing services to assist you.

Prospecting with Raffles
• *Try Your Luck*

"The harder I work, the luckier I get" ~ Samuel Goldwyn

Energize your database of past customers by making a raffle offer for a valuable prize explaining that if your customers can provide you with fresh referrals, they get chances to win a free gift. Remember, referrals have a high closing ratio. You can sell quite a few units from this type of raffle. You can give away items like:

• Televisions

• Movie tickets

• Dinner at a great restaurant

- Gift certificate for a shopping spree

- Baseball, Hockey, Football, Soccer, or Basketball tickets

Wherever possible, <u>partner with local businesses to provide prizes</u> and market to each other's customer lists. Just get creative and give away something of real value. If you continuously run these kinds of promotions every few months, your customers will always remember you and spread the word. Only a few people in automotive sales do this type of prospecting. Those who are doing this are very successful.

The prize needs to be significant enough to generate the interest and commitment for people to participate. Try this approach with your database of customers to see if the sales you get from the referrals pay for the promotion. You really only want to break-even because your objective is to generate additional customers to add to your fan base. Learn to give and you will receive.

Note: Local laws may limit what you can offer and how you can structure a raffle. Make sure you have your dealership's management onboard before launching such a promotion.

Forty-eight

Don't Use the "Getaway Pass"

. *Your Business Card has a Higher Purpose*

"Business cards are an effective networking tool for professionals" ~ Neil Kokemuller

If you have found showroom visitors asking for your business card just before they leave the dealership, **stop using your business card as a getaway pass**. Most salespeople will wait until the end of the conversation with the customer to hand out their business card. Why not hand them out <u>during the Meet and Greet phase</u>? Handing out your card at the end is an easy excuse for your customer to leave. So learn to work the "getaway pass" out of your system.

Visitors will also ask for <u>a brochure</u> as they are leaving the store. If your encounter with a sales prospect in the store ended this way, think about how you can turn the tables. <u>Use their request to get their email address</u> so you can send them an electronic copy and maybe a video. If you are frequently getting these requests, it's a sign that some aspects of your sales process need work.

Forty-nine

Lasting Impressions with Your Business Card

. *Use an Offline Device to Connect Online*

"What's your business card like? Mine has trumpet sounds" ~ Chris Brogan

All salespeople use business cards (usually supplied by your dealership) and, let's face it, they are generally BORING! If there is no reason to keep the card, most customers just throw it away. You must turn your business card into something creative and worth keeping so they won't forget.

Use an online service such as **Vistaprint.com** to create one yourself or get a friend with some design skills to assist you. Adding a picture is a good idea but also add a slogan that speaks to **your unique position in the car buying business**. Think about designing an <u>over-sized business card</u> that gives you space to include <u>places where you can be found online</u> (such as your Facebook address, LinkedIn profile, Instagram account, Twitter handle, your professional website address, etc.). Don't forget to include your cell phone number so you can be reached beyond dealership hours and so it's easy for contacts to text message you.

Use this <u>offline device</u> (a business card) to send people you have met to <u>your online locations</u> where they can learn more about you and your approach to business and where you can talk about how it is going to be to work with you.

Using the Internet & Social Media
• *Make it Easy to be Found Online*

About three-quarters of U.S. adults (77%) say they own a smartphone in 2017 ~ Pew Research

With about 80% of your customers and prospects now owning smartphones and researching all aspects of their vehicle purchase online, you must now have a presence online. In fact, *if you are not visible to potential customers online, you do not exist for all practical purposes*.

The more places you can be found online, the more chances you will be found by people in your area searching for a new vehicle. In **Step 48**, I talked about some of the basic online addresses where you should be visible and be telling your story. You do not need your own website but you can now have one set up inexpensively. If you are a good writer, **start a blog** on Google's Blogger platform and talk about topics of interest to your potential customers. If you are more verbal, set up your own car sales **YouTube** channel and use it to post video testimonials from your customers, walk around videos on vehicles on your lot, and helpful car shopping tips for those who have not yet met you in person but will start to get to know you when they come across you online. Building an online presence and profile is too large a topic to adequately cover here but it is the way you can work smart and create a definitive advantage for yourself.

Imagine your colleagues sitting around waiting for "ups" to arrive at the front door only to find that they are there to see you because they discovered you online. That's the power of building a position and a presence online in this digital economy.

Fifty-one

The Value of a Customer
• *Bonus Material to Get You Started*

"The customer's perception is your reality"
~ Kate Zabriskie

If you plan to be in this business long term, you need to adjust your mindset. You must understand the true value of a customer and the true value of each customer is their lifetime value. **Lifetime Value** is a concept you need to embrace and hang on to as a guiding principle. Sometimes we get so caught up trying to sell at sticker that we lose sales. Or worse, we neglect our past customers and miss out on the opportunity to <u>create an army of fans, supporters, and ambassadors for our business</u>. Building this following requires that you **make a habit of creating value for your customer**. In this context, building value means <u>finding every excuse to reconnect with past customers</u>; contact them from time to time via phone, email, text, direct messaging, newsletter, Facebook, LinkedIn, Instagram, etc. Use your dealership CRM (or your own spreadsheet) to keep track of family members, vehicles in the family, and keep that database up-to-date. Send congratulations on their car purchase anniversaries, birthdays, wedding anniversaries, special holidays, or just to say hello. Let everyone on your contact list know about new vehicles being launched by your brand, new technologies becoming available, and events at your dealership. Create a community that will provide you with a steady stream of business for life.

<u>How to Calculate the Value of a Customer</u>: Let's assume that you have <u>100 sold customers</u> and you are using all the strategies and techniques outlined in this guide. Do you think you could get 20 of them (20%) to provide one referral every year over the next five years? That's 20 vehicles each year before you do anything else. If you currently average 12 cars per month (144 per year), that's 29 additional deals in Year 1, another 58 in Year 2, and 116 in Year 3 (just from referrals). How much is that business worth to you over 5 years? Well, you would be getting 144 referrals in Year #5 (or 12 deals a month) before you started looking for any showroom or lot traffic.

Some Last Words
. *A New Way to Approach the Business*

Be Bold and Mighty Forces will Come to Your Aid

Canadian author **Basil King** (1859–1928) said, "***Be Bold and Mighty Forces will Come to Your Aid***". People are attracted to <u>confidence and enthusiasm</u>. Confidence and enthusiasm come from knowing your product and how it can help your clients solve their transportation problems. <u>Your customers want to give you a monopoly in your category</u>. They want to have someone in the car business they can trust and return to for advice and guidance. When you find a doctor, dentist, fitness trainer, plumber, golf coach, or real estate agent that you get to know, like, and trust, you want to keep them in your circle of contacts. If a friend asks if you know a good plumber, you want to have someone you can confidently recommend. So, don't sell yourself short. Make the bold gesture. Push the envelope. Some will criticize you but many more will be drawn to you. ***Your prospects and customers are looking for someone to lead them to a solution***. <u>Be their friend in the car business</u> for life and you will never have to chase business again. Good luck and good selling!

Gordon Wright
A Friend in the Car Business

If you want step-by-step guidance to learn how to master all these 50 strategies and TONS MORE to help launch your automotive sales career, then I urge you to immediately sign up at our website at http://www.ShowroomSalesSkills.com where you'll gain access to in-depth sales training information including templates, word tracks, and how-to videos that will start you on a path to success in the car business.

P.S. Stop making excuses and take action now! Don't delay any longer. Click on the link below to turn your automotive sales career into superstar success.

http://www.ShowroomSalesSkills.com

About the Author

When Gordon Wright found himself downsized following a successful 25+ year career in corporate marketing and sales, he decided to try selling cars and joined the team at a local dealership. He soon discovered that the way dealerships and car salespeople were generally conducting business was a lot different than the approach he had been used to in the corporate world. Having spent most of his life applying marketing principles to delivering customers to the front door, he was convinced that his key to success in this new environment would be to use his marketing skills and understanding of buyer behaviour to provide a different customer experience. Rather than chasing customers, he set out to orchestrate the flow of prospects to the dealership that were pre-conditioned, motivated, and pre-disposed to do business with him. At the same time, those who arrived "fresh" at the dealership were treated to a fresh new "no-objection" approach that made it easy to buy.

Gordon Wright pioneered **A New Way to Sell Cars** in the way he conducts business in the showroom and online. He was rewarded with a parade of repeat customers and referrals. Educated customers, he found, were happy customers and they were eager to spread the word.

In this training manual you will learn the principles and approaches he used to build a new and successful career in the car business. Ten years of working this system in the dealership showroom before, during, and after the global financial crisis (2007-2009) has proved that you can sell more cars and deal with fewer objections if you follow these *50 Steps to Showroom Mastery*. Now you know that this is *A New Way to Sell Cars*. It's time for you to reach your potential and *Discover How to Supercharge Your Car Sales Career and Become a Showroom Executive*.

www.ingramcontent.com/pod-product-compliance
Lightning Source LLC
Chambersburg PA
CBHW070944210326
41520CB00021B/7052